THE RIVER WHITE

A Confluence of Brush & Quill

Enjoy the Journey!

A river, though, has so many things to say that it is hard to know what it says to each of us.

—Norman Maclean
A River Runs Through It

FIRST EDITION, 2011

The River White © 2011
by Duane Hada & Ken Hada

ISBN 978-0-9833052-6-2

Cover Image: *Autumn Angler*
© Duane Hada, 2011

MONGREL EMPIRE PRESS
NORMAN, OK

ONLINE CATALOGUE: WWW.MONGRELEMPIRE.ORG

This publisher is a proud member of

Book Design: Mongrel Empire Press using iWork

THE RIVER WHITE

A Confluence of Brush & Quill

Watercolors
by
Duane Hada

Poetry
by
Ken Hada

MONGREL EMPIRE PRESS
NORMAN, OKLAHOMA, UNITED STATES OF AMERICA

Norman, Oklahoma
2011

from Duane Hada:

To my wife Marlene who shares my passion for rivers. I met her in a canoe and thought our Ozark budget honeymoon on the White River was the perfect way to start our journey together. Her love and faith in me and my art is the source of my inspiration.

To MeKenzie, my greatest masterpiece, a loving daughter who actually hangs my art.

Alex Cunningham, who traveled, explored and photographed the journey and put up with an artist to help make this a reality.

To Jim and Brenda Dugan, the ultimate patrons, who love the river and the art.

Jodie Smotherman who first helped me appreciate the sacred lands of the river from Ozarks to Foothills on its way to the Delta.

To Archie who shared her fishing spot and made me appreciate the culture and slower pace of life of the lower river.

To Roosevelt for his invaluable "plain air" critique of my art: "Dat's a fine damn good job ya do dare sur".

To the Float for Life Team who helped inspire the idea. True river rats with a devoted cause.

To Steve and Jo Wilson and all the White River land owners who graciously gave access through their property and the Wilson's dog Sally who felt my work wasn't complete until she made her mark.

To all those who appreciate and value original art and have allowed me to live my passion as an artist without starving.

from Ken Hada:

I would like to especially thank the administration and faculty research committee of East Central University, Ada, Oklahoma whose provision of a Professional Development Grant during the 2011 fall semester allowed considerable time to be applied to this project.

from Ken & Duane:

To Bill Parker, our guide, historian and conservationist of the White River Refuge. He is a living history of the lower White River.

Tate, duck guide extraordinaire, who braved the swollen Mississippi to make the last leg of the journey happen.

Lisa Gilley, who also grew up Ozark and loves her Boston Mountains and native roots, was invaluable in vectoring us to the source of the White River.

Kevin Pieper, a marvelous eye, who shares our belief that life, is not fully lived until one learns to see.

To those ancestral painters of the Far East whose main subject was a misty river rising above the land and who felt that a *plein air* painting was not complete without a poem to express it.

To our parents Gordon and Barbara who, by either fate or design, felt the need to raise their children close to clear Ozark springs and rivers. They instilled in us early a love for our Creator and for the land and the waters that carved it.

CONTENTS

for MeKenzie

A HISTORICAL PERSPECTIVE ON THE WHITE RIVER

By Gregg Patterson

The water is blue-green. You notice that right away. From a drifting hawk's view or a high bluff above the river, it looks like a stolen slice of the Caribbean Ocean. Long ago, it once was an ocean. Maybe it wants to be again. With that beautifully colored water, it's curious that early French trappers chose to call it *La Riviere Blanche* because of the purity of the water. Regardless, those captivating blue-green waters have been the boom to a few and the bust to countless more.

The White's source is deep in the Ozark National Forest. The best time to hunt for the source of this famous southern river is when the "turkey" trees are in bloom. The southern hardwood forest isn't fully leafed yet, its view still commandingly open; the bright white flowers of the dogwoods clearly marking the advent of spring's rebirth. A combination spring turkey and headwater hunt leads up the tallest peaks in the nation's oldest mountain range. At a present day 2,500 feet above sea level, you're on top of this part of the world that was once the bottom of an ancient sea, standing on sedimentary layers deposited over time like a layer cake during the Paleozoic Era. Unlike other mountain ranges that cry out in a bottom up birthing process of tremendous upheaval and natural violence, the Ozark Plateau, like a huge flat-topped salt block, remained after the seawater receded. The erosive action of flowing water deftly carved the Ozark Mountains top down as it slipped through cracks in the Pennsylvanian sandstone and shale

i

peaks down into the porous Mississippian limestone and deeper still into the depths of time made up of Ordovician dolomite. The weathering of water on rock created deep gorges, spectacular cathedral-like caves, underground passageways, claustrophobic cracks and sinkholes that have swallowed automobiles and houses. It's a Swiss cheese-like looking wearing effect known as Karst topography. The great streams of this region – War Eagle Creek, Kings River, Richland Creek, Crooked Creek, North Fork River, Little Red River, Buffalo River and Spring River in Arkansas; the Roaring River, James River, Bull Creek, Swan Creek, Beaver Creek and the Little North Fork of the White River in Missouri – all originate from the freshwater springs of the old sea bed. The White River's vast drainage basin – a jake leg plumbing system gone awry - is found in southern Missouri and northern Arkansas. It's the largest drainage basin in Arkansas covering more than 17,100 square miles.

The Osage Indians were the first historically witnessed humans to live and hunt in the White River Basin. (Little is known about prehistoric cliff dwellers that lived in the Ozarks before them.) Later when forced further and further west, Indians from other tribes lived off of the land in the Ozarks and along the White River. Like the white settlers that eventually pushed them out of the region, the Indians survived mainly off of the bounty of white-tailed deer, woodland elk, black bear, eastern wild turkeys, fish and the occasional buffalo. Deer, bear and turkeys were nearly wiped out by the Twentieth century following settlement. All now have strong populations. The science of wildlife management birthed at the turn of the century created deer refuges in the 1940s, restocked the Ozarks with black bears transplanted from Minnesota and Canada in the 1960s and trapped wild turkeys from Mississippi River islands and relocated them to these mountains to reestablish viable populations. The woodland elk is extinct but was replaced by the unsanctioned introduction of Rocky Mountain elk from Colorado in the early 1980s. Even the diverse warmwater fishery that was lost to the promise of modernization to this ancient mountain range when four hydro-electric dams completed in the early 1950s and

1960s went in on the upper White River (creating the Beaver, Table Rock, Taneycomo and Bull Shoals chain of lakes) has been replaced by a coldwater river fishery of non-native trout. It produces some of the world's biggest brown trout.

The tribes are scattered, the buffalo are gone. Science has no plans to rectify the situation.

The upper White River's famed trout waters begin in northwest Arkansas as it leaves Beaver Lake flowing north for Missouri. Trout fishing in the White River and its major coldwater tributaries like the North Fork and Little Red rivers is predominantly for stocked rainbow trout as there is little natural reproduction of this species in the river system. However, brown trout do successfully reproduce in sections of the upper White, as well as the Little Red River.

The upper White's cold waters run in the tailwater river sections for miles immediately below the dams. The longest tailwater stretch is the nearly 100 river miles of the White from below Bull Shoals Dam in Arkansas to Batesville. The fertile limestone water is rich in aquatic life providing an ample food base for trout. Their growth is rapid and provides a world-class trout fishery on certain sections of the river and some of its major tributaries. A six-inch tagged stocker brown trout taken three years later from the Beaver tailwater section of the river had grown to more than 10 pounds. Annual average length growth rates of four to six inches on the White and seven inches on the four-mile North Fork River tailwater are testament to the river basin's potential to grow huge brown trout. The stretch below Bull Shoals Dam consistently yields 20-pound browns annually and the occasional 30-pounder. Previous all-tackle world record brown trout of 38 pounds, 8 ounces and 40 pounds, 4 ounces have come out of major White River tributaries the North Fork River and the Little Red River respectively. Browns of this size are only consistently rivaled in the world by the sea run browns that migrate into the rivers of Patagonia at the southern tip of

South America and in the Great Lakes and its tributaries; those fish having a far greater range of habitat and food resources to access.

As inextricably as the White River is tied to the Ozark Mountains and its colorful settlement history, the upper river leaves the ancient hills on its way to eventually become part of the ocean again flowing into the flat sediment-rich Mississippi Alluvial Plain. Its clear blue-green color replaced by the brown silt-laden waters so influenced by the whims of the much larger Mississippi River.

The history of the lower White River is one of a working river where first steamboats and now barges, trains and trucks carry the bounty of floodplain farms that were born through the massive clearing of the bottomland hardwood forests of oaks, cypress and gum trees. "King" cotton, rice, soybeans and other row crops dominate this rich, fertile land. The clearing of the bottoms ushered in what is now Arkansas's leading economic engine – agriculture. Vast agricultural fields spread out on either side of the river as it leaves the foothills just west of Newport until it loses itself in the remnant bottomland hardwoods of White River National Wildlife Refuge before meeting the Arkansas River.

River rats have commercially fished, hunted and trapped the lower White River since settlement. To experience the river fully, it's necessary to visit the people who live in houseboats there. Sit down, and eat the river. Feast off of plates of fresh-caught buffalo ribs and succulent White River catfish, cornbread, fried green tomatoes and sweet iced tea. The people here move to the rhythm of the river. They prefer answering only to it. It's in the refuge that the river floodplain takes on its former dark, swampy self. Some of the state's biggest whitetail bucks die of old age here. Turkeys are abundant and the original native White River black bear still survives here. Spring floods replenish the refuge's numerous and colorfully named oxbow lakes – Hole-in-the-Wall, Escronges, Red Cat, Brown's Shanty - providing great fishing, and the backwaters are stained the color of tea. The diverse songbird population is magnificent, and duck hunting here in the deep woods can be a religious experience.

And then it ends.

At the bottom of the refuge, nearly 700 river miles from its beginning, it ends. Losing itself into the Arkansas River and then quickly merging into the Mississippi headed to the Gulf of Mexico.

The White River is dynamic, chaotically structured motion, timelessly sliding downhill from its source high on a mountain peak at the bottom of an ancient ocean, restlessly trying to become what it once was. We are but brief witnesses to its task.

The heart of God
bleeds pure
springs upward – as
all good things
rise – so this gift
multiplies a
universe of time.

A river begins
and we will follow,
we will marvel
together – the birds
and I, broken limbs,
fallen leaves –
hands of God.

And will you travel
with us too?
You can – if you
learn to see, if
you listen and
promise to leave
her unblemished.

You cannot see
700 miles until you
muse the bubbles
before you. Truth
is more than what is,
but also, what
likely will be.

I see your beauty but
I would not have imagined
your power, such grace
flowing 700 miles.

It is easy to mistake
appearances. Often we need
to be reminded of depths
below the surface,

that a story, a life of stories
lies hidden, yet we tend
to judge only *Now* –
the close surface,

the easy view lazy
eyes first see. Remind us
that a beginning matters –
such substance

from a modest Ozark
creek – where sand
and rock hold gentle water
even fools consider.

3

Already the bluffs are tall,
protruding white
from a green forest.

How can pain withstand
limestone memories
glistening in pale sun?

Therefore, we need red
canoes – to give white
rocks celebrity due them.

So much depends on red
canoes, on blue water
purling past white rock,

over beige sand. A wooden
oar fit firmly in a
grasping, upturned hand.

5

See the fishermen
lining the ripples

mending to a spot
they see, a spot

that allures them,
holds them entranced

beneath seraphic sky,
these votaries flush

with line and fly,
shriveled in attention.

All my life I've heard
the name Bull Shoals
and still I feel what
I felt as a child
upon hearing.

Say it with me
audibly, ardently:
BULL SHOALS –

Just the sound evokes
awe, if not fear.

Only a fool tries
to master what
is bigger than life –
Herons statued
in fog – know better.

A man dares to enter
God-space, mystic
dark ignoring pale hearts.

Be honest now – you
feel what you cannot name,
you fear to articulate
what you feel –

This dark moment
permits you to pretend
you're ahead of the game,
passing others –
such is the myth
of the purple-hearted.

11

We're just wildflowers
blooming on a
sandy bank.

We're a lustrous bunch
giving the world
some color.

We're fortunate now
to flourish while
sun shines on

nurturing water.
We live this dream –
why won't you?

13

The Greeks liked
the number
three. Christians

borrowed this,
attempting
to put a

face on In –
finity.
Pagans and

pilgrims, all
of us, merge
into one –

and fly flights
of wispy
clouds, screech the

litany
of blissful
Kingfishers.

15

Walk like a Heron
Walk like a Heron

my brother tells me
as we sneak into

flat water to cast
a green soft hackle

without ripple.
Walk like a Heron

fish like a Heron
– live like a king.

17

I've often said
In my next life
I want to be

a bird. I want
to soar, to dive,
to dally as

Eagles falling
in ecstasy
from heights unclaimed.

19

We always fish this run
after noon, after
working ourselves blue
at other places –

Then evening comes
slipping on smooth stone
our bent rods know
how blue good can be.

21

Mark my journey:

I know I'm getting close
now, closer to satisfaction,
a stasis of soul that comes
only with persistence –
even grim slippery steps
yet Time passes. A train
rolls round the mountain.
Dreams, like rivers, are forged
in valleys of desire.

23

This place is so lovely,
so vital, even God
is humbled to be close by.

On the hottest days
your heart (and other
organs) cringes in icy pain

as you force yourself down
below the surface
burning fierce with purity.

You rise gasping, grasping
– drops of healing glistening
the back of your neck.

Of course changes
round us
into humans – not

machines. Magic
light streaks
promise warmth to us,

A covenant
we keep
with life-causing sun.

27

I'm envious. I wish
a particular bend
in this river bore my
name, held my story – a
secret that Daisies share
as they return each May.

History is not just
past events. Even now
you and I are making
history by the way
we live along these shores,
by the way we return.

29

You bend both ways
if you're a major river.

You are too strong
to be confined to one course.

Like a great snake
you roll over and let a

gossamered sun
soothe the coils of liberty.

31

I always feel
like I'm on top
of a world here

like teetering
at the edge of
things unnamed
a place unmapped.

The first Fall hues
forecast splendor
unsurpassed –
the world over.

33

If I were truly Buddhist
I would set aside pen and paper
to let silence write me.

What words shall I use?
What is gained by talking?

I have long felt the ghosts here
both content and riled:
One for the location, the
other – because far too many
of us refuse them.

Wake Up!
I tell myself.
Wake up
to *phthalo* past
the point of speech.

On some days goodness
and mercy are not
merely abstractions.

Gravel slips between
your toes, a crawdad
scrambles out of your

way – backward – as you
push forward until
paradise finds you.

On some days rain
is welcomed, on
others we whine.

    If we were wise
    we would accept
    blue on black, drops

        in a river.
        Are you worth more,
        really, than Elm

    leaves shuffling
    in wind? Ferries
    were used by men

to transport their
economy
as bards float words

    but in truth it
    is the river
    that moves us – drops

        of destiny –
        so much more than
        mere metaphor.

Someone borrowed
the meadow
made fertile by floods.

A sentinel Pine
makes me think
this is enough.

Some knobs cannot
be cultivated
nor lived on

but by the wildest
life, the life
we dare not tame.

41

I feel I should apologize
for my part in the lie
that is often called progress.

But I promise to disturb as
little as I can from now on,
a severe promise to keep.

Wild gifts endure nonetheless –
not to pretend my failure doesn't
matter. Oh no, it's not that at all.

Maybe what I love most
about rivers is how
they bend together
toward some mystic
whole we imagine.

Confluence is a lovely
word, a word that implies
sharing, getting along,
making new space
from disparate parts.

No atom, no action exists
alone: water joins
water joins tree and
plant, sand and soil,
grass and flower.

Even the Mayfly
that emerges, but for
a desolate moment
only to die, plays his
part to perfection.

45

The lucky ones
tie john boats
to a fading red

dock, then lean on
warped poles fixed
to tattered wood slabs.

They hear tapping
tin, water
lapping in the breeze.

They swallow stale
beer before
napping their tired lies.

47

Can you imagine
violent coughs of coal
smoke lingering above
a bruised iron cage, men
trying their damnedest
to go upstream?

Forever, we have been
going upstream, which is
to say, forever we've been
going the wrong direction
– a river knows, even
as a river flows . . .

I've caught Smallmouth here
along with the Trout. I'm sure
the folks before the damming
of the river knew this. In some
ways, we must be governed.
We fail to regulate ourselves,
but our medicine is much the
same now as then: Slip out
across those long stone slabs,
cast into shadows falling on
the rocky shore – and hang on!

When we were boys
the town of Calico Rock
held mysterious sway
over us. The place

was unique, marked
for all to see. Our
journeys downriver always
confirmed it so.

I notice today dappled
reflection mirrored on
the water – the same
as it always was – amen.

Do you see the tracks
in the soft shallows
where life has preceded
you? There is much
to learn from those
who trekked before us.

I wonder if Sumac turning
meant as much to them
as it does to me? We are
downstream – nearing
the foothills, and I know
what red leaves mean.

55

How many blues
can you make me?
How long till I know

the myriad that frames
my existence?
I am shadowed

though I bathe in sun.
We live the rays between
pigments of history.

I turn away.

Is it to see
what kind of fool
disrupts Eden?

Or are some things
too stunning
for my eyes?

Well, yes – of course.

59

Crossings are the stuff
of life. We must move.
We cannot be constrained.

All our days are rehearsal:
pray our time to cross
occurs not at floodstage.

61

Here I can hide.

It is not my concern
that a Great Spirit knows me
– that is above, beyond me.

My goal is to stay unfound
by the human hunter –
wretched hound who assails

my heart. Without merit
my stone-cold soul relishes
a few stolen moments

in this pristine sanctuary
where water assuages
my secret with song.

The company we keep
spends our days
like Oak leaves
that refuse to fall
clinging with stubborn
beauty – as long as
possible – to all we know.

We live in the afterglow
of death. Our friends,
a family, a johnboat
and the trees that give
us hope – all this coming
to us through rhythm
that sings Autumn.

Rivertowns display a
common trait:
relief born of survival.

Maybe desert hubs
know similar fears, but
here, water is the

killer and the savior.
So folks dance like
fractured incandescent

bulbs glowing hopeful
yet cower with astigmatic
vision. We live

as we die – in the
triumph of now – refracted
as ghosts always are.

If winter
　　　always comes
do we not feel
　　　certain
our bareness
　　　is destined?

There is a time
　　　of yellow
that none of us
　　　can deny
a leafless day
　　　water mourns.

I have journeyed far,
my life's canoe seems
spent, feels flexed, old

But an end is not yet.

These tired oars, scarred by
use, rise and dip in
disciplined measure.

I prayed for an easy life,
but now repent of such softness.

How could one seek escape
from harshness that turns
rogues into pilgrims?

Now I pray for life to settle
as water naturally does,
– catfish on a cane pole
and memory to tell it all.

73

If you go with me far enough,
you will recognize yourself
swinging through the coils of
time – a heart snaking in goodness
does not always know itself –
this is why you must go with me,
why we all must go together.

75

Forked sticks are evidence
of hunger, the substance
of things unseen.

I am not moved
by whirling traffic above me,
I only watch a tight line.

Here, posited, as family
before me, I partake
in the ritual I am.

Someone decided
here is the place to set
up and that decision

remains. Wild birds
adjust, but I'm not sure
I can or should. Would

you? If I am lucky,
I might just catch my
Grandpa's catfish –

the one that broke his
line all those years ago.
There's better line now.

Even the name suggests
irony: clear, certain –
yet I cannot walk here
without getting mud
on my boots, moisture
seeping, claiming me.

Generations of murky
men have climbed clover
hills about the river –
just to get a better view.

81

I've spent a lifetime tending
this old pole. Some days
it's as good a friend as can be

— one worth depending on,
bending in slack water, a
peculiar place God put me,

a spot where Heaven's fish
swim past this here muddy bank
just to feed my tired bones,

just to tell a wearisome soul
not to quit her journey,
to claim the light of day.

Birds at sunrise
sprinkle this Cypress
forest with song.

These last woods
sanctuary a beauty
overlooked.

Warbler and Nuttall
– golden residue of
sustaining floods.

See how a swamp
survives, how forgotten
colors flourish.

It's hard to believe
the same water
that left Pettigrew Mountain
brings me to this point.

This seems to be
a different river altogether
but then that's how
we fool ourselves.

There is one current
in us, keening
beneath various faces.

I will drop anchor
(hardly necessary today)
and bait a hook and wait.

I know this much psychology:
I need to get my rod bent.

Looking back
from where we've been
the silver surface

blurs with phosphorescent
clouds. Unclear lines
cover Devilish currents

lurking, but I would not
trade this conversion
for gold or fame – I

can not imagine life
without a journey.
Something happens deep

inside when the power
of a continent floods
the dream of a tender heart.

A world is cut –
an artist molding tomorrow
with a grain of sand.

A Sycamore leaf
floating – slowly
now – but never still

I remember near
the source, floating
down from a branch

above water. In some
forgotten field I saw you;
I followed you

all the way but
you are not yet finished.
The Mississippi

will carry you home –
home – to mother sea –
the everlasting sea.

DUANE HADA'S *plein air* paintings are pure artistic responses that seem to flow effortlessly in a medium that many artists struggle with. This comes from a life time of observation, critique, and a strong work ethic. His painting outdoors frees him of the technology trappings and aides of the studio. It's old school, just a blank canvas, a trained eye fueled with a strong passion. Like a maestro at the piano, Duane sets up his field easel and a rhythm of ease and melodious application of color comes out. He instinctively extends the brush and strikes a color note and the music begins. Lifelong keen observation of his native landscape has created a seemingly effortless connection that flows from eye to hand, palette to canvas. Many marvel at the confidence and speed with which Duane paints. When asked how long does it take to do a painting Duane often responds, "a lifetime."

As an avid fly fisherman Duane brings a unique, aesthetic appreciation to the sport of angling. Duane credits his life-long passion as artist and angler to being raised close to nature in the rural Ozarks' Buffalo and White River country. Growing up surrounded by some of God's greatest handiwork fuels the creative inspiration that has blended beautifully into a career as both angler and artist. Duane has traveled and painted extensively throughout trout country as well as to several saltwater destinations and he enjoys recording both angling and fish species of the areas. He paints both in the studio and *plein air* to capture the light and essence of the moment.

Duane Hada completed his BSE in Art at the University of Central Arkansas, Conway in 1985. He regularly teaches painting and drawing classes as an adjunct professor at Arkansas State University in Mountain Home, Arkansas. He holds painting workshops locally through his White River School of Fine Art, and travels to teach. Duane is one of the founding members of the White River *Plein Air* Painters group.

Rivertown Gallery, Duane's studio and guide service, is located in Mountain Home, Arkansas. When asked about his vocation, he'll quickly tell you some days he's an artist who guides, and some days he's a guide who paints. Either way, his clients cherish their memories of a great days spent on the water.

KEN HADA is a professor in the Department of English and Languages at East Central University in Ada, Oklahoma where he directs the annual Scissortail Creative Writing Festival (held each April) and teaches courses in literature and humanities. He completed his Ph.D. at the University of Texas-Arlington in 2000, writing on Cormac McCarthy's *Border Trilogy*.

In addition to his scholarly work in ethnic literature, western regionalism and ecocriticism, Ken has two books of poetry in circulation: *The Way of the Wind* (Village Books Press, 2008) and *Spare Parts* (Mongrel Empire Press, 2010). *Spare Parts* was awarded the National Western Heritage Award from the Western Heritage Museum and Cowboy Hall of Fame for outstanding book of poetry. It was also a finalist for the Oklahoma Book Award, and four of his poems from that collection were featured on Garrison Keillor's nationally syndicated radio program, *The Writer's Almanac*.

GREGG PATTERSON is a longtime outdoor and environmental journalist and has been a columnist for *Sports Afield*, Trout Unlimited's *TROUT* magazine and for ESPNOutdoors.com. In 2003, he received the Jade of Chiefs Award from the Outdoor Writers Association of America for lifetime achievement in conservation communications. He continues to hunt, fish and explore the natural wonders of the White River from its source to its mouth. Patterson is a graduate of the University of Missouri's School of Journalism where he also earned a Masters degree in Science.

93